REALLY, REALLY BIG QUESTIONS

about Space and Time

KINGFISHER
LONDON & NEW YORK

Copyright © Kingfisher 2010
Illustrations © Nishant Choksi 2010
www.nishantchoksi.com

Published in the United States by Kingfisher,
175 Fifth Ave., New York, NY 10010
Kingfisher is an imprint of Macmillan Children's Books, London.
All rights reserved.

First published in 2010 by Kingfisher
First published in paperback in 2012 by Kingfisher

Consultants: Alison Boyle, Curator, Astronomy and Modern Physics, the
Science Museum, London; and with additional thanks to Jonathan Chase.

Distributed in the U.S. and Canada by Macmillan,
175 Fifth Ave., New York, NY 10010

Library of Congress Cataloging-in-Publication data has been applied for.

ISBN: 978-0-7534-6747-3

Kingfisher books are available for special promotions and premiums.
For details contact: Special Markets Department, Macmillan,
175 Fifth Ave., New York, NY 10010.

For more information, please visit www.kingfisherbooks.com

Printed in China
1 3 5 7 9 8 6 4 2
1TR/1111/UTD/WKT/140MA

REALLY, REALLY, BIG QUESTIONS

about Space and Time

Mark Brake

Illustrated by

Nishant Choksi

CONTENTS

CHAPTER 1
RECIPE FOR A UNIVERSE

CHAPTER 2
GOODNESS GRACIOUS, GREAT BALLS OF GAS!

CHAPTER 3
TIME, TIME, AND TIME AGAIN

CHAPTER 4
THE GREAT BIG FUTURISTIC SPACE ADVENTURE

INTRODUCTION

WHAT ON EARTH IS GOING ON UP THERE?
MARK BRAKE

Maybe tomorrow, or maybe a decade or a century from now, scientists may make the most shattering discovery of all time: evidence of alien life. What kind of space and time would these aliens inhabit? Where would they call home?

This book contains many questions such as these—questions that will stretch your brain and make you think.

Have you ever looked up and wondered, "Is there a map of the universe?" or "Why is the night sky so dark?" While waiting for a bus, have you asked yourself, "Does time always go at the same speed?" Or have you wished you lived on another planet and pondered, "Do aliens look like me?" All of these questions are asked in these pages, as well as many more.

Before you read these questions and the answers I've given, let's make one thing clear. While many of these questions have straight answers, many of them do not. Or they might have answers that will *change* in the future.

These questions are all "scientific." Science is what we call "cumulative." It sort of rewrites itself as new things are discovered and new ideas are formulated. Our ideas about things change as time goes by, so at any one time science can only really be thought of as:

"THE BEST CURRENT INTERPRETATION OF THE NATURAL WORLD."

You and I are designed for the purpose of living on Earth, which is a planet— a part of the cosmos, the universe. But you and I are also *a part* of the universe. We are made of the same materials that can be found on the other side of the universe. Those materials may not be assembled in the same order, but they are basically the same.

So we can try to understand the universe from this point of view, from the planet Earth, and build ideas about what things might be like "out there." But we can't touch, taste, see, hear, and *feel* everything in the universe close-up. At least, not yet.

Once you've read these pages, you'll be tempted to think, "So, is that it? Have we finally grasped what the universe is like?" But the answer to that is *probably not*. In fact, to even *suggest* that we understand the universe is very *un*scientific. Science is all about questioning things—*all the time*. Even when we think our ideas are correct.

Who's to say that people won't look back and laugh at our ideas about the universe one day? So the golden rule is *Don't just listen to me—the universe is right there in front of you . . . Take a good look for yourself.*

1

RECIPE FOR A UNIVERSE

BANG! And so the universe began.

Many people think that a huge *explosion* of space and time, known as the big bang, created the universe. But the universe as we know it is not fixed—it is *changing* all the time. It is changing right now, while you are reading these words.

And few things are changing faster, it seems, than our understanding of it. The more we learn, and the more questions we ask, the more the secrets of the cosmos seem to slip through our mortal fingers . . .

But that's no reason to give up. Let's keep on asking those tricky questions.

WHY
DO WE THINK THERE WAS A
BEGINNING
TO THE UNIVERSE AT ALL?

From Earth, there are approximately 5,000 stars that you can see with the naked eye, and here and there you can make out the odd, hazy smudge of a galaxy. A galaxy is a huge swarm of stars, very far away in deep space, made up of billions and billions of stars.

When astronomers observe the light from these galaxies, they find that the light is more "red" than it should be. When this happens to light, it's known as "red shift," and it means that the galaxies are moving away from us.

Now, it's not just one or two galaxies that have this "red-shifted" light . . . it's all of them! Billions of them, in fact!

If all the galaxies are moving away from one another today, that means that at some point in the distant past they were all in the same place . . .

That's why we think there was a "beginning" to the universe.

WAS EVERYTHING

COOKED
up all at once?

Those big, bright balls of light we call stars are in many ways the building blocks of our universe.

Stars are made mostly of hydrogen, which they burn for millions and billions of years. So, most of the universe that we see is made up of mega amounts of hydrogen. About 74 percent of it, in fact. Almost 24 percent of the universe is helium, so that leaves just 2 percent for everything else that exists . . .

All this hydrogen and helium was cooked up right at the beginning of the universe, or so we think. The universe likes to keep things simple, and hydrogen and helium are as simple as it gets for stuff. Everything else was cooked up *inside* the stars, for many generations after the beginning of the universe.

That means that almost everything else you see on Earth is made of what we might call the *heavy stuff*. Yes, the carbon in your skin, the iron in your blood, and the gold in the World Cup trophy—these were all cooked up by stars over the course of history.

WHEN DID THE UNIVERSE START?

Nothing ever happens "immediately." This is because light takes time to reach the human eye (even though it is traveling at a speedy 186,000 mi., or 300,000 km, per second). So, as you watch your cat getting its head trapped in the refrigerator door, that actually happened the tiniest fraction of a second ago.

So, in a way, your cat is time traveling.

For this reason, we can think of stargazing as a form of time travel.

Our universe is so unimaginably vast that from its outer limits, light takes longer than twice the age of Earth to reach our telescopes. And because it takes so much time for light to travel across these huge distances in space, everything in the universe has a *look-back time*.

The farther out we look, the further back in time we are gazing. And since the look-back time for those outer reaches of the universe is around

13.75 billion years, we use that measurement to mark the very beginning of time.

HOW **ON EARTH** CAN WE DESCRIBE THE UNIVERSE FROM **HERE?**

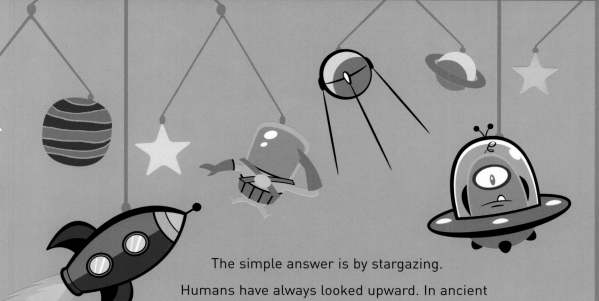

The simple answer is by stargazing.

Humans have always looked upward. In ancient times people used to judge the seasons, and the rotation of crops for food, based on the movements of the sky. And for centuries, people used the stars to navigate their ships.

Stargazing was an important part of life. And it still is today.

When we watch the night sky, everything seems to revolve around Earth. By night, stars, planets, and galaxies rise in the east and set in the west. By day, the Sun rises in the east and sets in the west. So it's easy to get the idea that we are at the center of everything!

Aha! But then we found out it's just an illusion, caused by the fact that Earth turns around on its axis as it travels around the Sun.

Astronomy—the scientific study of the universe—has taught us that Earth is not at the center of the universe. Nor is it likely to be the only object of its kind or made of materials only to be found on Earth. Not even the Sun is that special. The Sun is not at the center of the universe, nor is it the only star with planets around it, and now we know that it will not keep burning away in the sky forever.

So, how about the Milky Way, our galaxy? No! That's not at the center either. It's just one of 100 billion other galaxies, all adrift in an ever-expanding universe, which we have discovered using our telescopes. Heck! There may even be other universes. Who's to say this is the only one?

It's amazing, when you think about it, that all these discoveries have been made from this one point in space—planet Earth—which is an extremely tiny ingredient in the grand recipe of everything.

HOW DID WE EXPLAIN THE UNIVERSE

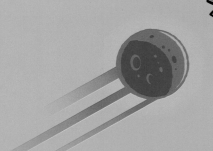

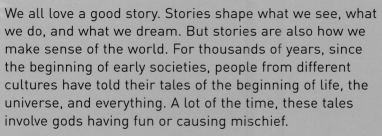

We all love a good story. Stories shape what we see, what we do, and what we dream. But stories are also how we make sense of the world. For thousands of years, since the beginning of early societies, people from different cultures have told their tales of the beginning of life, the universe, and everything. A lot of the time, these tales involve gods having fun or causing mischief.

In one story, which comes from West African culture, a giant sky-serpent-god moves his 7,000 coils, which form not just the hills and valleys of Earth but also the stars and planets of the universe. When he sheds his skin in the Sun, it releases all the waters over Earth. Then the reflection of the Sun in the water creates a rainbow.

Beautiful!

Another tale of creation, told by the native North American Kiowa Apache people, sounds like the world began with soccer. The story begins with darkness. Suddenly, from out of the darkness comes a thin disk, one side yellow, the other side white, and the disk hangs in midair. A small, bearded man then emerges, and soon a tiny brown ball—not much larger than a bean—is kicked around by the gods until the ball expands to the size of Earth . . .

BEFORE SCIENCE came ALONG?

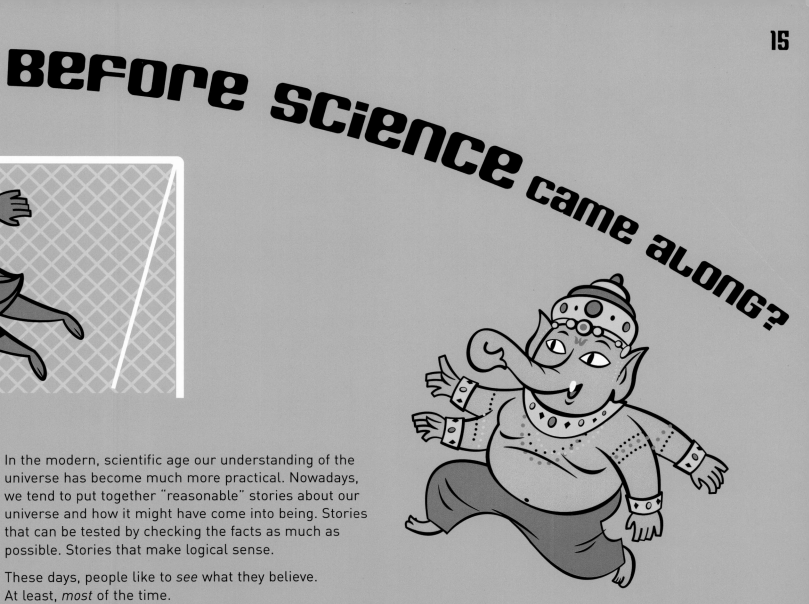

In the modern, scientific age our understanding of the universe has become much more practical. Nowadays, we tend to put together "reasonable" stories about our universe and how it might have come into being. Stories that can be tested by checking the facts as much as possible. Stories that make logical sense.

These days, people like to *see* what they believe. At least, *most* of the time.

Sure, it's still okay if you want to believe in any of the creation stories that have emerged from religions or popular mythology over the centuries. Who knows—any one of these theories of creation might be correct! As I said right at the beginning, *don't take my word for it.*

BRAIN BURN!

The ancient Greeks named the universe after their word for "harmony" (*kosmos*). Do you think they chose the right word?

DOES THE UNIVERSE FOLLOW A RECIPE?

Imagine you wanted to take a chunk of the universe, like grabbing a handful of soil from the ground. And imagine you wanted that chunk to be just like any other chunk of the universe. In other words, you wanted it to be a "typical" chunk so that you could use it to make a repeatable "universe pattern."

To do this, let us imagine the most gigantic ice-cream scoop of all time.

Using the scoop, we're going to scoop up that "average" chunk of universe. How big is this chunk going to be? It can't be solar-system-size because our solar system is probably not the same as others. And it can't be galaxy-size because our galaxy is just not the same as other galaxies.

Astronomers have figured out that the typical chunk you'd need to scoop to get all this "average stuff" in the universe is about 300 million light-years across! Only then could we say that we had spotted a truly typical chunk of what the universe is "like" in other, distant parts of it.

HOW DO WE MEASURE
THE UNIVERSE?

Light is the fastest thing known to science, but it still takes time for light to cover the vast distances across the universe, from one object to another. So—as we've already said—we see things in space as they were in the past. The farther we look out into space, the further we look back in time.

So using *time* is actually a pretty sensible way to measure distances in space . . .

The journey of light from the Moon to Earth takes about one second. We see the Moon as it looked a second ago, so the Moon is one "light-second" away. We see the Sun as it looked about eight minutes ago, so it's eight "light-minutes" from Earth.

Other stars are much farther away. Even the next-closest star to Earth, Proxima Centauri, is about 25 trillion mi. (40 trillion km) away. Light takes more than four years to travel from that nearby star and hit the naked eye. So it is four "light-years" away. We are looking at a four-year-old image of the star.

IS THERE A MAP
OF THE UNIVERSE?

Maps of space are very tricky to make because all the stuff in the universe is constantly on the move and the distances involved are huge. In deep space, unlike on Earth, you can't visit places to draw maps in detail. You have to make guesses by reading and measuring the starlight that comes to Earth.

The largest and most up-to-date maps of space are called red shift surveys. These are the biggest maps of the universe that we can get. They show that galaxies are formed into immense clusters and separated by enormous voids of nothing. That's why astronomers call the large-scale map of the universe a "cosmic web."

WHAT IS THE UNIVERSE MADE OF?

The universe is basically made of two types of stuff. Stuff you can see, and stuff you can't.

We know a good bit about the stuff you can see. It's what makes up planets, moons, stars, and galaxies. All these things either give off light or reflect it. Stars shine, and planets and moons reflect starlight. And galaxies are made up of millions and millions of stars, so they shine, too.

But recently, astronomers discovered that a sizable portion of the universe is missing.

It seems that all the "light matter" (planets, moons, stars, and galaxies) is just the tip of the cosmic iceberg. Scientists believe that a lot of the *rest* of the universe is made of some exotic, mysterious material known as "dark matter" and a baffling phenomenon called "dark energy."

Dark matter is the stuff we *cannot* see. It is, in a sense, the shadow of the universe.

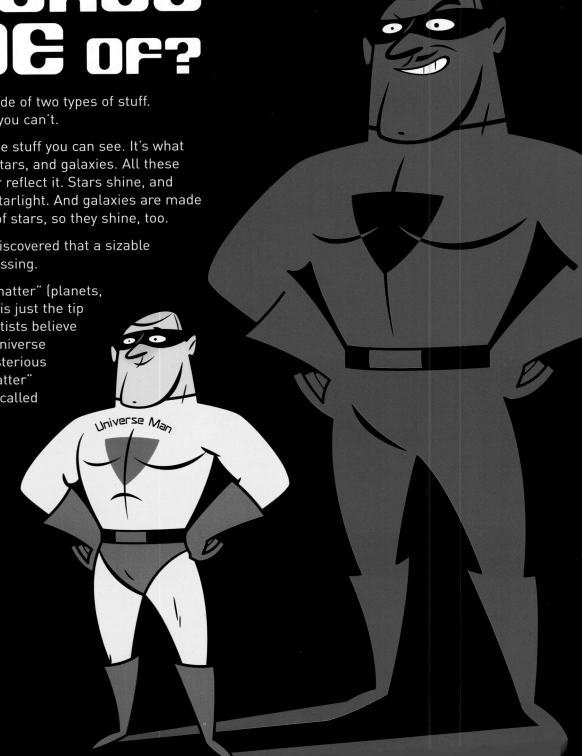

Universe Man

WHY IS THE NIGHT SKY so DARK?

The sky is blue during the day and dark at night. How come it is so *moody*?!

Sunlight is multicolored, and the air scatters blue light more than red, so the sky is mainly a cool blue color during the daytime. By evening, with the Sun lower in the sky, blue light is scattered out completely, so sunsets (and sunrises, too, for that matter) are often a warmer red color.

But why is the night sky dark?

Okay, the Sun is facing the other side of the planet, so we're not receiving its light. But the universe contains simply billions of stars, in all directions. So why isn't the sky a dazzling *white* at night?

There are two parts to the answer. First, the light from stars and galaxies is traveling to us from all sorts of different distances across the universe, so it does not reach us at the same time. Second, these objects are all of different ages, so the older ones will be dimming while the newer ones are shining brightly.

With me so far?

The result: at all times there is light from very distant objects that hasn't reached us yet and light from nearer objects, which is either dimming or shining brightly depending on the age of the stars and galaxies.

That, in a nutshell, is why the night sky is never filled with light.

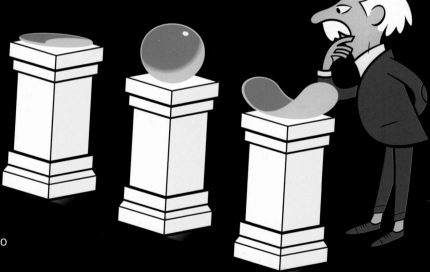

WHAT SHAPE IS THE UNIVERSE?

Everyone's heard of Albert Einstein, right? He's the guy with the wild, white hair who rewrote the rules of science early last century.

One of Uncle Albert's big ideas was this: mass bends space. Yes, that's right! The mass (amount of "stuff") of something in space actually bends the space around it. And the more mass you have in one spot, the more curved that "space spot" becomes.

Einstein also got to this big question: if space can be *bent* by mass, then how might this affect the overall shape of the universe?

In other words . . . If you think about this space-bending business on a larger scale, could the overall mass of all the stuff in the universe give it a *curvy* shape?

We may never know for sure. But space experts do think there are THREE possible universe shapes: flat, spherical (ball-shaped), and hyperbolic (saddle-shaped).

IS SPACE SMELLY?

That very much depends on where you stick your nose.

Astronomers scouring the heart of our Milky Way galaxy recently found that huge clouds of stuff are floating around there—the kind of stuff from which life on Earth is partly made. Not only that, but they think this stuff would taste a little like raspberries . . . and smell like rum.

It's a big discovery because it means that planets being formed at the galaxy's heart will already have some of the stuff vital for the development of life.

Other scientists, working at NASA, have also been banging their brains about smells in space. When they interviewed astronauts about what space smells like, they were told different things by different space people. Some said space smelled like fried steak. Others spoke of hot metal. And others even said it reeked of welding a motorcycle.

After all this, it's a little bit of a disappointment to find out that this delicious space meal of hot metal soup (for a starter), fried steak (main course), and rum 'n' raspberry ice cream (dessert) will not be savored by most astronauts. For one thing, the heart of the galaxy is a very long way away. And for another, most people don't have a very good sense of smell or taste while in space.

"Two things are infinite: the universe and human stupidity; and I'm not sure about the universe."

Albert Einstein (1879–1955)
theoretical physicist

IS THE UNIVERSE GETTING FATTER?

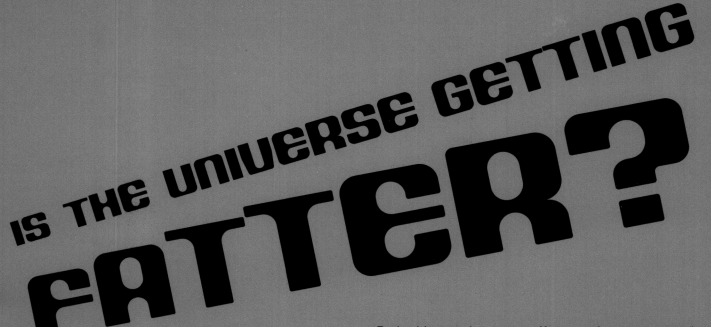

By looking at the way stuff moves in space—you know, star systems and galaxies and so on—we can try to figure out whether the universe is still expanding from the original "big bang."

We think there was a beginning to the universe, and we know that its galaxies are moving farther apart into a seemingly "endless," infinite space . . . So now we've been trying to figure out if this expansion is getting faster or slowing down, and if and when it might stop. In other words, it seems that the universe has been getting fatter and fatter for a very long time—so when is it finally going to go on a diet?!

The latest news is rather exciting.

Astronomers say that the expansion of the universe *is* getting faster and faster. That means the space between the galaxies is getting even bigger.

If this *accelerating* expansion continues, over millions of years, all the galaxies beyond our own local group will be so far away that it will be hard to detect them. It will seem as though, one by one, the lights in the sky are going out.

In that case, the future of the universe is not necessarily bright. It could even be quite dark.

Spooky.

2
GOODNESS GRACIOUS, GREAT BALLS OF GAS!

It's time to rub shoulders with the true celebrities of the cosmos. Let's meet . . . THE STARS!

Brown dwarfs, red giants, white dwarfs, blue supergiants, black holes, yellow dwarfs, super-dense neutron stars . . . They're a colorful bunch, huh? There are billions and billions of them out there, and just like people, they are all individuals, with different types of personalities. Stars are like A-list actors in Hollywood: they can be kind of difficult at times, but there would be very little action without them.

HOW CAN THE SUN

Normally, the Sun is too bright to look at, let alone try to judge its size. But picture yourself on a crisp, foggy morning. There's little to see in the sky, but you can just make out a big ball of dim light. This is our Sun. You marvel at how huge it is.

That faint ball of light is 93 million mi. (150 million km) away. Let's say you have a flying car, and let's say you whiz off toward the Sun at 93 mph (150 km/h). Don't worry, there are no speed limits in space, except this one: nothing travels faster than the speed of light. The Sun is so far away that even at 93 mph (150km/h) it would take you a million hours to get there (that's 114 years).

Even though the Sun is this far away, it still looks huge to us from planet Earth. That's because it's 864,000 mi. (1.4 million km) across! That's fat enough to fit 109 Earths across its middle, and well over one million Earths inside it.

BE A DWARF?

Just to go once around the Sun—assuming you could stand the heat and that your car was up to it—you would have to fly at supersonic speed, nonstop, for 227 days.

Okay, you get the picture. The Sun is **BIG**. But compared with some stars, it really is pretty tiny. In fact, in the words of modern astronomers, it's a "dwarf star."

Let's take just one example. In the constellation of Orion, there is a supergiant by the name of Betelgeuse. If you could pick up Betelgeuse and plop it where the Sun is, in the center of our solar system, it would swallow up the orbits of the four innermost planets—Mercury, Venus, Earth, and Mars. Now that's big.

WHAT MAKES SUNSHINE?

The Sun is the key to life on Earth. Without it, there would be no light, no heat, no food to eat, no weather, no days, no seasons, no Earth as we know it. In fact, no solar system at all because the Sun drives everything that happens here.

And the Sun does all this by sheer power. It is a ball of fiery energy that burns about 4 million tons of gas per second. That's as much energy as 7 trillion nuclear explosions every second. No wonder it's so incredibly hot!

Because the center of the Sun has a temperature of about 28.8 million °F (16 million °C), it's hot enough to turn hydrogen into helium. So one of the Sun's main jobs is making new atoms. It is an atom-making machine that lights up the entire solar system with sunshine power.

Scientists believe that the Sun has been doing this job for about 4.57 billion years. In all that time, it has been a constant energy-giving star, sending out massive amounts of light from Solar System Central.

And it's not just in our solar system that sun power is crucial. Stars power our entire universe. *Let there be light!*

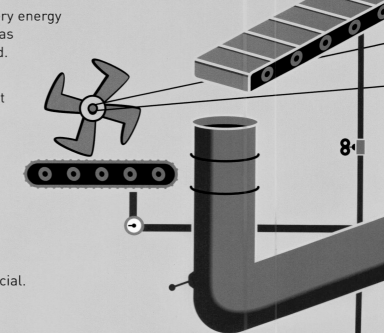

DO STARS MAKE NOISE?

The ancient Greek thinker Pythagoras thought that the Sun, Moon, and planets made music as they moved through space, though he *didn't* think it was something you could actually *hear*. And medieval mathematician Johannes Kepler was certain that the planets were spaced out from the Sun in gaps that had something to do with musical scales.

But this "music of the spheres" is not just mystical nonsense. Oh, no. Today's astronomers take great interest in the different sounds that stars make.

When they "listen in," they hear a regular, repeating pattern. This tells them that a star is pulsating, or throbbing, in space. The different sounds give astronomers information about the star's inner workings, its age, size, and the stuff that's in it.

Of course, the astronomers cannot listen to stars *directly*. They have to convert the "seismic waves" (vibrations) from stars into a form that humans can hear on Earth. It's a little like being a "space doctor"—slapping a big stethoscope on a star and giving it a health check!

Au

He

Si

DO STARS LIVE FOREVER?

Stars need fuel to keep going, so they spend their lives desperately seeking stuff to burn.

For most of their lives, these Sunlike stars burn hydrogen, turning it into helium. When stars *run out* of hydrogen, some astronomers think that they just switch to helium and burn that instead. In fact, stars can burn carbon, neon, oxygen, and silicon, too.

When a star uses up one type of fuel and changes to another, it sends out a warning: it swells up massively in size to become a *red giant*.

In the distant future, our Sun is expected to become a red giant, expanding to 200 times its normal size. When that happens, astronomers expect it to swallow up the inner planets of the solar system, including our beloved Earth!

But don't worry. It seems that Mars will survive, so we'll just have to move and become Martians.

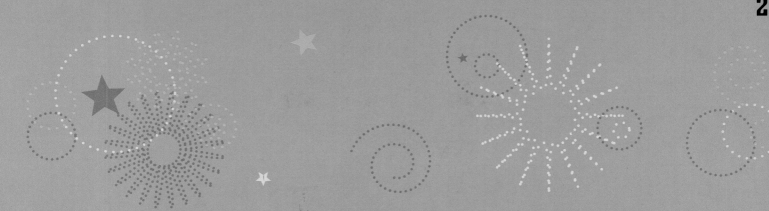

DO STARS EXPLODE?

And then some! An exploding star is called a supernova, and it is extremely powerful. A supernova can release more energy in one minute than is released by all the normal stars in the entire universe during that very same minute.

Star explosions like this happen to very big stars. When they run out of fuel to burn, these big guys blow up.

The burst of light that they give out as they go supernova can be as much as our Sun emits over its entire lifetime. So it's easy to see how a supernova can often outshine the entire galaxy in which it sits.

Astronomers think that there is a supernova—in a galaxy the size of ours—every 50 years or so. So it's truly a very special firework display for stargazers!

WHY DO SUPERSTARS LIVE FAST and DIE YOUNG?

Stars come in many sizes and many masses. Mass is a measure of the amount of stuff that something contains. The mass of a star tells you how much gas is in it.

The smallest stars have about 100 times more mass than Jupiter. (This means that if Jupiter had been 100 times more massive, it would have been a star and not a planet.) The biggest stars are thought to have a mass about 100 times greater than the Sun's. These fellows are real monsters, but they don't last long.

The bigger the star, the shorter its life.

Monster stars have lifetimes that last in millions, not billions, of years. That's because they have a ravenous appetite and burn up gas like there's no tomorrow. And they have a habit of exploding.

But it's the little guys that count. These little ones are about as massive as the Sun, and some have less mass. There are many more tinies than there are monsters, and they have "forever lifetimes." A star with half as much mass as our Sun will continue burning for many billions of years.

IS ANYWHERE
COMPLETELY
DARK?

Sometimes, a star gets so amazingly massive that it cannot stop collapsing in on itself under the pressure of all that mass! This may happen because the star has too little fuel left or because it is picking up a lot of extra stuff from somewhere close to it in space.

Having huge mass means exerting a lot of gravitational pull on surrounding things. So it could be that a massive star's gravity is attracting everything near it—including light—and stopping everything from escaping its massive pulling power.

These massive stars appear black, so astronomers like to call them black holes.

Aren't astronomers clever with words?

Black holes could be the darkest places anywhere in space. The trouble is, these things are so *completely* black that it's hard to actually find them.

DO BLACK HOLES TURN YOU INTO SPAGHETTI?

Our feet stay on the ground because Earth has a lot of mass, which has a gravitational pull on us (who have less mass). The closer you are to a massive object, the more its gravity is exerted on you.

Now, black holes are supposed to have LOOOOAAAADDDDSSSSS of mass. So much mass, in fact, that the difference in gravity exerted on your head and on your toes would be huge! This would have the effect of stretching your body into long, thin shapes—rather like spaghetti.

The name that astronomers give to this stretching effect is *spaghettification*. (I told you they were clever with words.)

The spaghettification stretching power is so immense around a black hole that resistance is futile (useless!). But don't fret too much yet. It's unlikely that anyone will be taking a peek into a black hole in the near future . . .

WHAT'S IN THE CENTER OF THE MILKY WAY?

I'm sure you are now worrying about being turned into spaghetti. Worry not. Astronomers have found good evidence of black holes existing, but not in planet Earth's backyard! However, one of the key candidates is right in the middle of our own Milky Way galaxy.

Don't panic! That's about 26,000 light-years away, so it's hardly likely to swallow up Earth next Wednesday.

There's a lot of matter—or mass—in the center of the Milky Way, and in a relatively small amount of space. It's exactly the kind of conditions where a black hole would thrive. So much so that astronomers think there is an enormous, *supermassive* black hole lurking there.

In fact, they think there may be supermassive black holes in the center of most galaxies.

WHEN STARS DIE, WHAT HAPPENS TO ALL THEIR STUFF?

Listen, stars never really die. Many just slowly change into a different kind of star, and some explode to leave behind a ghostly relic of themselves. It all depends on their size, or how much matter they have.

Remember, the smaller the star, the longer its life.

Small stars live for billions and billions of years. And when these little fellows do eventually run out of fuel, they continue shining for a long time afterward. When small stars get to this stage in their lives, they're known as *white dwarfs*. Astronomers think that more than 97 percent of the stars in our galaxy will end up like this.

The monster stars are rare, and they have a different story to tell.

The midsize ones become *red giants*, swelling up in size and changing color as they go.

Big stars go bang in a supernova, and then they become either black holes or *neutron stars*. Neutron stars are amazingly dense—as dense as the entire human population of Earth squeezed down into the size of a sugar cube.

Now isn't that *sweet*?

So, there are different life journeys a star can take. Each journey has an endpoint, and those endpoints are the white dwarfs, red giants, neutron stars, or black holes. Whichever way they go, stars are always blasting out stuff into space, stuff richly made of the chemical elements created inside the stars.

That leftover "star stuff" is then part of the universal mixture—part of the recipe for a new generation of stars to be made out of the old.

It's the ultimate in recycling!

WHAT'S THE DIFFERENCE BETWEEN ME, A PLANET, AND A STAR?

You are made of star stuff. Sounds crazy, but it's absolutely true.

The carbon in your skin, the iron in your blood, the calcium in your teeth—these elements are just some of the stuff cooked up inside stars and then ejected into space to make new stars, planets, and other things such as people.

Take carbon. It's an element on Earth that's important to all life. Carbon is made in stars of all sizes, but it is not burned up by them. It survives the starry furnaces and is released, along with other elements, as the star itself goes through a sort of recycling process toward the end of its life. It is then free to make up parts of other stuff—like us!

Astronomers can tell what's inside stars by reading the starlight that eventually falls to Earth. These experts used to think that there was a big difference between stars and planets. But these days they think of them as one great big family of stuff.

At the beginning of our own solar system, everything formed at the same time from a collapsing gas cloud. The four small, *inner* planets—Mercury, Venus, Earth, and Mars—are mostly made of rock and metal. But the four *outer* planets—Jupiter, Saturn, Uranus, and Neptune—are largely composed of hydrogen and helium gas, just like the Sun itself.

So what makes a star so different?

Stars shine, and planets don't—that's the main difference. There are planets and stars of various sizes, masses, and fillings. But the big distinction between a large planet such as Jupiter and a star such as the Sun is that Jupiter *just isn't quite massive enough* to get the hydrogen gas burning at the very heart of itself.

BRAIN BURN!
Human beings are the product of a grand and cosmic recycling program in space. *Groovy!*

WHAT IS LIGHT?

Light is traveling energy.

When you do a cannonball into a swimming pool (possibly not allowed by the lifeguard), the energy created by your body hitting the water can be seen in all the waves moving across the water. The important thing is that the water wave is not made up of water. The wave is made up of energy. And it is the *wave* that does the moving, not the water itself.

Light is also energy that travels in waves, although it can travel through space as well as through a substance such as water.

You can think of light as "packets" of energy, called photons, which our eyes are able to see. There are lots of different ways to produce photons of light. In space, the photons that travel to us as starlight are created at the very center of stars—such as our Sun—that burn up hydrogen gas.

HOW QUICK IS LIGHT?

It's the quickest thing in the universe!

Light moves at a speed of about 186,000 mi. (300,000km) every second. Because we know this, the speed of light is a useful way of measuring big distances in space.

Light is so swift that it can go around Earth's equator ten times every second. It can then jump over to the Moon from Earth in a second or cruise to the Sun in eight minutes.

It could be a very neat way to travel, if only you could jump on a light beam.

(Please don't try this.)

But distances in space are so huge that even light takes more than four years to get to the next star (after our local one). And light would need about 100,000 years to get across our Milky Way, which gives you a pretty good idea of just how enormous our galaxy is.

IS WHAT I'M SEEING ACTUALLY THERE?

We can see things in space either because they are *emitting* (giving off) light or because they are *reflecting* it. We know that this emitted or reflected light is often traveling great distances to get to us and that this journey might take a very long time.

So . . . some of the things that you see in the night sky may no longer be there!

Imagine a star went bang somewhere in our galaxy in a really bright, supernova explosion. And imagine that it was so far away that it took light from that star about 100,000 years to reach Earth. Even though the supernova was brilliantly bright, we wouldn't actually see the explosion on Earth for 100,000 years *AFTER* it took place.

In all that time, in between the explosion and us seeing it, we would be gazing up and looking at a star that was not actually there anymore. Crazy!

3
TIME, TIME, AND TIME AGAIN

I suppose it must be time to talk about . . . TIME!

We all think, rather smugly, that we've got a good handle on time. As human beings, we've decided how to "measure" time. We "read" and "tell" the time, all the time. But where did time *come from* in the first place?

It doesn't take much to confuse us once we really start to investigate it. What if time sped up, or slowed down, or decided to go backward? What if there were holes or gaps in time? Then we really would be all over the place.

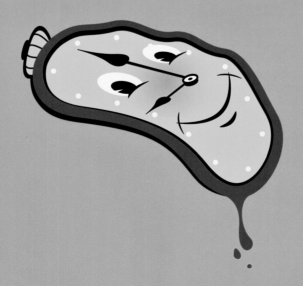

HOW DID WE PUT TIME TOGETHER?

Okay, so you can't exactly "build" time. But we measure time in a way that suits our experience on the planet: the time it takes for Earth to rotate once around its axis is what we call a "day" (24 hours). The time it takes for Earth to travel once around the Sun is a "year" (365 days).

But the bigger *story* of time has been more difficult to piece together.

When the Industrial Revolution came along (in the late 1700s) and we started digging in the ground to look for fuels, engineers discovered the fossilized remains of many animals in the rocks. Animals such as the dinosaurs, which no longer live on Earth.

Our story of Earth's origin suddenly started to change. The remains of these extinct creatures were found in crazy places—sea creatures on hilltops, polar bears at the equator, and elephants on the Moon (okay, so I made up the last one). Planet Earth must have gone through big changes, both to its rocks and to this host of bizarre beasts, to explain all the things that were being discovered.

So, instead of thinking that Earth and the universe formed around 6,000 years ago, people started to realize that it must have taken millions and millions of years for all of Earth's changes to happen.

HOW DO WE KNOW THE AGE OF THINGS IN SPACE?

So, scientists realized that it had taken millions of years for the changes in the rocks and the animals to take place, and this led to huge changes in the way people thought about time. People began to understand that the whole universe around us was incredibly, amazingly old.

The scientists figured out how to date the rocks on Earth by measuring how long it takes stuff in the rocks to waste away. This helped us discover that our little planet is truly ancient, at an age of 4.5 billion years.

In the 1960s and 1970s, *Apollo* astronauts visited the Moon and brought back rocks. These rocks turned out to be the same age as rocks on Earth. This was also true for meteorites and for pieces of Mars that had fallen to Earth. So they must have been created at the same time.

Astronomers are also estimating the age of the Sun using computer models. They think that it's even more ancient than Earth, at about 4.57 billion years of age. And this makes sense. After all, you can't have a solar system without the Sun setting up home there first!

IF A WARDROBE HAS 3 DIMENSIONS, WHAT IS THE 4TH?

A wardrobe is an object with three dimensions, which describe the space it is occupying—its height, its depth, and its width. But your world also has a *fourth* dimension. The first three dimensions are space. The fourth is *time*.

Let's think about that wardrobe again . . .

You probably think you know exactly where your wardrobe is going to be a week from Wednesday. But, even though you don't notice it, your wardrobe is constantly moving. Sure, it's always in that dusty corner of your bedroom. It doesn't move in terms of space. But that's only *three* of the four dimensions, isn't it?

In terms of time, it's a different story.

Take another look at your wardrobe. Is it moving? No? Are you *sure*? *Definitely* not moving? Actually, it is. It is moving in space-time. It's staying where it is in the three dimensions of space, but the *fourth* dimension of time is changing.

So—even though you are not seeing this happen, that fourth dimension is most definitely there.

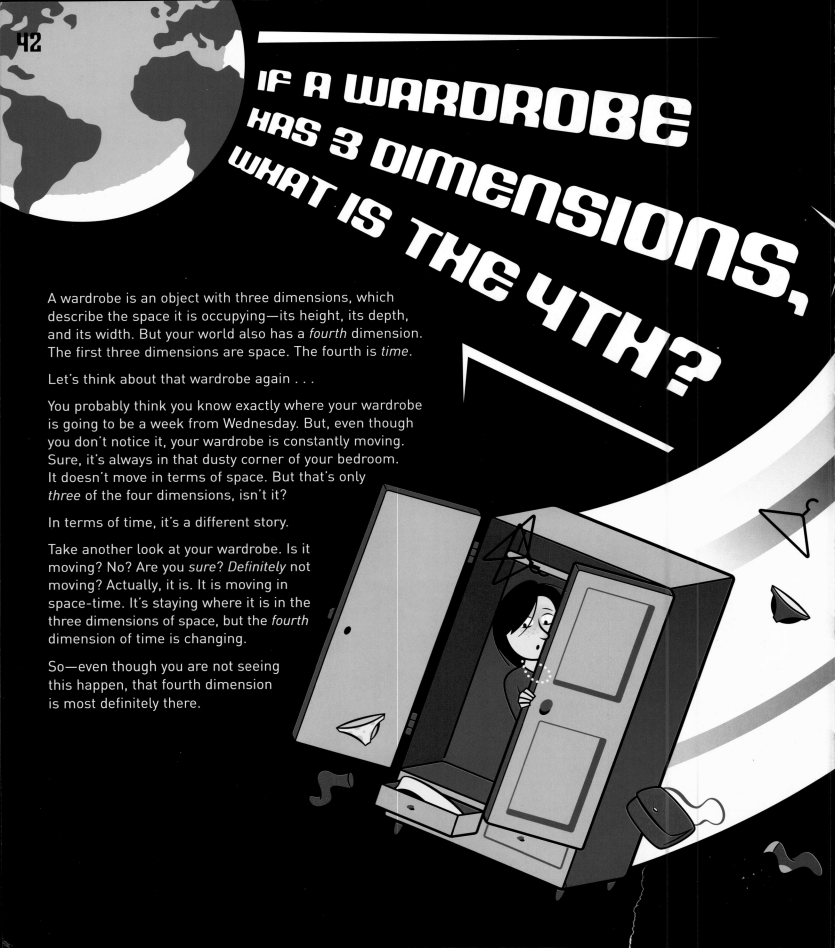

DOES TIME ALWAYS GO AT THE SAME SPEED?

It's easy to get the impression that time always flows at the same rate because mostly it seems to, in day-to-day life. But, in fact, there is no such thing as *THE* time, a flow of time that is the same throughout the universe.

Remember Einstein? (Yes, the guy with the wild and wacky white hair who rewrote the rules of science . . .) Well, he showed us that our day-to-day understanding of time is wrong. Time is not "absolute." It is "relative." This means that the rate at which time flows depends on where you are and how fast you are traveling.

For one thing, moving clocks run more slowly than stationary ones. This is true—even if you use the most accurate clocks in the world, known as atomic clocks.

Imagine that you have two of these "atomic" clocks. You put one onboard a spaceship, and the other stays at home on Earth. And imagine that the spaceship whizzes off to a nearby star system at half the speed of light.

When the spaceship returns, the atomic clock on Earth says 30 years have gone by. But the clock onboard the spaceship says the total journey time was only 26 years.

It seems incredible, but only because we assume that the two clocks tick at the same rate. But they do not!

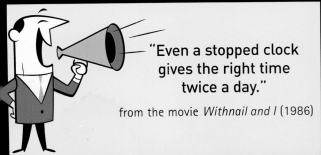

"Even a stopped clock gives the right time twice a day."

from the movie *Withnail and I* (1986)

HOW IS MY BODY LIKE A CLOCK?

Strangely, people don't always age at the same rate. It's not just mechanical and atomic clocks that are affected by speed. It's *biological* clocks, too, such as the aging of your own body.

Here is a story of twin brothers . . .

Just after celebrating their 21st birthday together, one of the twins (an astronaut) goes on a long trip into space, traveling at 96 percent of the speed of light.

It makes sense that if the astronaut is away for 14 Earth years, he will be 35 years old on his return to Earth. As the astronaut descends the stairs of the spaceship, he naturally assumes that his twin brother is also 35. So, as you can imagine, he is pretty horrified to discover that his twin brother is actually 71 years old.

This puzzle is a real-life effect of traveling in time and is known as the Twin Paradox.

Although we have never tested this effect using real people, we know that it is true. The facts have been checked using atomic clocks, flown in airplanes traveling at different speeds around Earth.

IS TIME THE SAME ON BIGGER PLANETS?

Time is not the same on different planets.

To see why, take our little planet, for example. Time on Earth passes at different rates in different places. And all this weird time business partially depends on the strength of gravity in these different locations.

Imagine yourself in two different places on planet Earth: a sunny beach and on top of Mount Everest.

The sunny beach will be closer to the heart of the planet, and that means the pull of gravity (toward the center of Earth) will be greater in this location. Because of this, clocks will run *slightly* more slowly here. On top of Mount Everest, the pull of gravity is weaker, which means that clocks will run a little faster.

Once again, the facts have been checked by those hard-working scientists using highly accurate atomic clocks. The clocks that were sent up to high altitudes, where there is less gravity, showed marginally faster times than the clocks on much lower ground.

Gravity is stronger on fatter (more massive) planets, which means that clocks would run more slowly there. So it is true. Time itself would be slower.

Goodness.

HOW DO YOU BUILD A TIME MACHINE?

If there's one thing in this great big universe that you cannot mess with, it's time. Science-fiction writer H. G. Wells knew this only too well. So he went and messed with it. In 1895, he wrote an amazing novel about time travel called *The Time Machine*.

After all, if you can move around freely in space, why not also in time?

Imagine you have your own time machine, delivered brand new to your door. Where first? The last days of the Roman Empire? The Middle Ages? Or to the very end of the universe itself? The Middle Ages. Good choice.

Okay, let's look at the instructions carefully . . . Temporal camshaft. *Check.* Fourth-dimensional perambulator. *Check.* Ignition. *Check.* Ignition?! Hang on a minute. Exactly how are these time machines supposed to work?!

If you want to build a time machine to travel into the future, you need a spacecraft that can move pretty close to the speed of light. As the spacecraft approaches this speed, time moves more slowly. Once you get back to Earth, you will hardly have aged. But decades, or even *centuries*, will have passed "back home."

Bingo! You've arrived in the future.

Traveling backward in time is even trickier! To do that, you would need the kind of machine that works using the mind-warping, time-tinkering technology of wormholes . . .

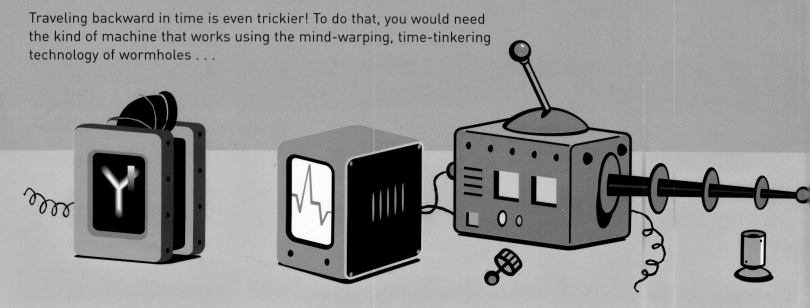

ARE THERE HOLES
IN SPACE-TIME?

One of the "least impossible" ways to travel in time could be the wormhole, a theoretical region of space-time that is *warped*. It is a potential "shortcut" in space and time through which we might be able to travel. Many astronomers think that wormholes might exist, but they have no evidence of them just yet.

But there may be snags. Imagine you create a wormhole. And imagine you're just bursting to journey back in time to dote on a *Diplodocus*. Set the dial for the Jurassic!

But hang on. You would not be able to travel back in time to a date *before* the wormhole was actually created. This may explain why we've never been overrun by tourists from the future. We haven't had the technology to create a wormhole. Not yet.

Unlike a black hole, which is a one-way journey to nowhere, a wormhole has two mouths—an entrance and an exit—and they are joined by a single "throat," or tunnel. Stuff may "travel" from one mouth to the other by passing through the throat. We haven't observed a wormhole yet, but the universe is still young. And we haven't been looking for very long.

If astronomers can just find a way of keeping a wormhole throat open, some think it could be turned into a cosmic time machine. **Wow.**

The amazing
TIME-O-MATIC
Making your time-travel
dreams a reality!

4

THE GREAT BIG FUTURISTIC SPACE ADVENTURE

Coming soon to a theater near you . . . THE FUTURE!

We experience the future all the time—or, at least, our idea of what it might be like—through books, movies, television, and so on. Why are we so obsessed with it?

It's the outward urge! Space is a vast, *vast* expanse, and as human beings, we can't wait to discover what lies beyond our known limits. We see our future "out there." We are *itching* to get out into space, make it our own, and find out all we can about it.

But how will this change our relationship with the universe? Will it make us any more a part of it? Or will it make us feel even more alone than we did before?

Much later, in the early 1600s, came the invention of the telescope. Italian astronomer Galileo Galilei was pretty handy with this exciting new instrument. He discovered four giant moons around Jupiter and that our Milky Way was made up of thousands of stars. And when Galileo spied the Moon, he saw mountains and craters not unlike those on Earth! When Galileo wrote about his discoveries in 1610, he urged his readers to imagine . . .

What would it be like to walk on the Moon?

Galileo's awesome discoveries inspired writers to imagine what life might be like in space and what it might be like on another planet. And so science fiction truly began in the way that we know it now. The first "sci-fi" stories were about space travel. They imagined sailing out into space, and the first destination was (yes, you've guessed it) the Moon.

WHERE DID SCIENCE FICTION BEGIN?

Listen, humans haven't always been fascinated by the future. We haven't always had an urge to sail out into space, the final frontier. But we have been curious about the cosmos for a very long time. You *could* say, in fact, that science-fiction writing began with early mythological stories or with the early theories of the ancient Greeks.

BRAIN BURN!

What if science-fiction writers really did have the power to "write" the future?

WHO INVENTED SPACE TRAVEL?

Sometime between 1620 and 1630, astronomer Johannes Kepler wrote a book called *Somnium*. Kepler was probably the most important astronomer in the world at the time. He was a smart guy. He believed that space travel would be possible one day. And he knew that we'd have to beat Earth's gravity to get to places such as the Moon. In Kepler's tale, lunar demons travel between Earth and the Moon on a "bridge of darkness." It sounds fantastic! But here's the neat part: the bridge carries travelers out into space, to a point of "special gravity" where they can just drift down to the Moon's surface. If only it were that simple in real life!

Another early sci-fi work was *The Man in the Moon*, written by a Welsh bishop, Francis Godwin, and published in 1638. Bishop Godwin also understood that the first problem of space travel was gravity. In his tale, a traveler uses a flock of geese to travel to China. But instead, he accidentally ends up on the Moon.

In 1660, the world's first science organization—the Royal Society—was founded in England. Its members decided that a space voyage to another world was, in fact, a very real possibility. And the rest . . . is history!

WAS
NEIL ARMSTRONG
A MODERN
COLUMBUS?

It's a story of exploration.

Long before the invention of the telescope, the world was a place of travel and trade. As maps became more accurate, ships stopped creeping along coastlines and started taking off across the oceans. Tenth-century Vikings settled in America, and Christopher Columbus (1451–1506) rediscovered it about 500 years later. This was like finding another "world" on Earth, just as Galileo went on to find other worlds in space.

Galileo's telescope was a kind of ship. It took him, and all the other onlookers on Earth, to places in space nobody had ever imagined. The telescope brought the Moon to life and made it *real* in our minds. It became a reachable place—another *world*, close to our own.

We began to think about the possibilities: Are there aliens on the Moon? What would it be like to walk over that craggy landscape?

The long journey to Neil Armstrong's "one small step" on the Moon, in 1969, began with Galileo and the telescope in 1609.

WHO OWNS SPACE?

Yaargh! Let's hark back to the days of pirates on the high seas. When they raided ships, they wouldn't search for gold, silver, or pieces of eight. *Oh, no.* They would head straight for the hold—where the ship's maps and clocks were kept. The most valuable cargoes were the tools of science, the tools of *discovery*.

So, why is science so valuable?

Navigation and seafaring have always been important for trade. If you can discover something and sell it to the rest of the human race, you can make a lot of money.

Spacefaring may also bring fame, fortune, and bounty!

Earth's natural resources are beginning to dwindle, so it's no wonder that its nations dream of sailing out to distant worlds—to plant a flag on them and say, "Okay, that's ours now!" Owning a moon or an asteroid where there are lots of natural fuels and materials could be worth an absolute *fortune*.

But it's worth remembering that space travel is an expensive business. A big investment. You'd have to put in a lot of money to plant your flag on another planet, say. And there's no guarantee that you'll get anything back.

And just because you've landed on another object in space, does that really mean that you can call it your own? Surely that's rather cheeky!

After all . . . who owns planet Earth? Maybe it's aliens, and we're all working for *them*.

ARE THERE ALIENS in OUR SOLAR SYSTEM?

Today's space missions to Mars look for water, among other things. For where there is water, there might be life. In 2007, caves were discovered on Mars, so future missions may go there to search for Martian life under the ground . . . But the robotic explorers will be looking for tiny bugs, not bug-eyed monsters!

Another possible home for alien life is Europa, one of Jupiter's biggest moons. Europa is smooth and completely covered by an icy crust. *Underneath* that ice, the giant moon may be hiding a vast underground ocean—and tiny microbes, similar to those in Earth's oceans, may be lurking in those subterranean seas.

ARE THERE OTHER EARTHS?

In 1543, a very important book was published, written by a Polish astronomer named Nicholaus Copernicus. This book suggested that the Sun, not Earth, was in the center of our small solar system. Before Copernicus, people did not think that Earth was a planet. They thought it was . . .

(BIG FANFARE) THE CENTER OF EVERYTHING IN THE UNIVERSE.

Ever since Copernicus, astronomers have been wondering about other planets like ours. Since the 1800s, we've known that most stars in the sky are like our Sun and that many of them have planets in orbit around them. Such planets are called "extrasolar" planets. It was only in the 1990s that we found the first official example. But today, we know of more than 300.

We haven't found another Earthlike planet yet. But space is *gargantuan*. We've found that there are more stars in the universe than there are grains of sand on all of the beaches on planet Earth. And many of those billions of stars will have planets in orbit around them. Surely there must be another place like Earth out there somewhere . . .

DO ALIENS LOOK LIKE ME?

Here's the thing: if Earth's not the only planet out there, and there are life forms on other planets, then Earth's not so special after all. It's just another place where life is possible.

And here's another thing: biologists such as Charles Darwin started thinking about how creatures on Earth change over time—how they evolve. But his ideas about evolution don't just work for creatures on Earth. They work for aliens, too. Creatures on other planets would also need to change and evolve to suit the environment in which they live.

Since the huge majority of extrasolar planets are nothing like Earth, it makes sense that aliens wouldn't look like humans. It would be very spooky if there were another "you" out there in space!

IF SPACE IS FULL OF ALIENS, HOW COME THEY HAVEN'T VISITED US YET?

This question is known as Fermi's Paradox because it was posed by the Italian physicist Enrico Fermi.

And it's a very good point. If intelligent life is out there, why hasn't it made contact with us yet?

First, space is mind-bogglingly big. Intelligent aliens have probably noticed this whenever they've thought of popping down to Earth for a takeout pizza. Maybe space travel ain't that easy. Heck, we've only managed to visit the Moon in the past 50 years of so-called "space exploration," and that's only one light-second away!

Second, perhaps they are watching and waiting. Waiting until we evolve a little more, get a little smarter.

Once we've evolved, maybe they'll come and invite us over for coffee, to join in with their intergalactic chitchat and exchange wild tales of universal exploration.

Third, maybe all the smart aliens have never bothered with technology and travel. Maybe they are happy just plodding around their planet, gathering and hunting, like hunter-gatherers are supposed to do.

And finally . . .

Maybe we *are* being visited. All the time. That's why people have spotted UFOs, flying saucers, and believe that they have already enjoyed that steaming cup of coffee (and maybe even a slice of cake) up on the aliens' mother ship.

WOULD ALIENS WANT TO STEAL OUR STUFF?

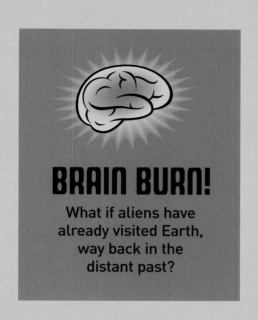

BRAIN BURN!

What if aliens have already visited Earth, way back in the distant past?

Isn't it funny, the way we always imagine aliens to be super intelligent?

Okay, fair enough. If they've jetted across the furthest reaches of space for a pizza, and we can only manage to reach the measly Moon, maybe they ARE smarter than us. But if that's true, what would they want with Earth stuff? Imagine an alien fumbling with a toaster, filing its nails with your skateboard, or trying to figure out why you only have two shoes.

Ah, but maybe they've run out of resources. Like us, perhaps they have a growing population that they find difficult to feed and water. But if they're THAT advanced, they're hardly going to jet halfway across the galaxy looking for wood. They would probably look for raw materials in their own solar system, closer to home.

GLOSSARY

Words in **bold** refer to other glossary entries.

ARMSTRONG, NEIL (Born 1930) An American astronaut who was the first person to set foot on the Moon, in July 1969, and one of only 12 human beings ever to do so. Armstrong was the commander of the *Apollo 11* mission to land two men on the Moon.

ASTRONOMER A scientist who specializes in outer space, including the Sun, Moon, planets, stars, galaxies, and space objects.

ATOM A basic unit of matter. The word *atom* comes from the Greek word *atomos*, which means "uncuttable."

ATOMIC CLOCK An extremely accurate clock, which works by using the natural behavior of atoms as its timekeeping element.

AXIS An imaginary line around which a three-dimensional object, such as a planet, rotates. Earth's axis is the imaginary line that runs through the inside of the planet, from the North Pole to the South Pole.

BETELGEUSE A red **supergiant** star in the **constellation** of Orion. Betelgeuse is the ninth-brightest star in the night sky.

BIG BANG A theory of the beginning and evolution of the **universe**, which is supported by current observations. The theory says that the **universe** began about 13.75 **billion** years ago and continues to expand to this day.

BILLION One thousand **million** (or 1,000,000,000).

BIOLOGICAL CLOCK A roughly 24-hour cycle in the natural behavior of living things, including plants and animals.

BLACK HOLE A region of space from which nothing, including light, can escape. Astronomers think that black holes are made by very, very dense matter causing a massive warping of space-time.

COLUMBUS, CHRISTOPHER (1451–1506) An Italian navigator and explorer whose voyages across the Atlantic Ocean made Europeans aware of North and South America.

CONSTELLATION An area of the night sky used to refer to a pattern of prominent stars, which appear to be close to one another.

COPERNICUS, NICHOLAUS (1473–1543) A Polish astronomer who was the first in modern times to suggest a Sun-centered solar system, moving Earth from the center of the **universe**.

COSMOS From a Greek word, *kosmos*, which means "order" or "harmony"—the opposite of chaos. It is still used as another word for space or **universe**.

DARK ENERGY A supposed form of energy that is spread through all of space and which tends to increase the rate the **universe** is expanding.

DARK MATTER An invisible form of matter that is thought to make up the vast majority of **mass** in the **universe**. Though it cannot be seen, the existence of dark matter can be guessed at by the behavior of visible, or "light," matter.

DARWIN, CHARLES (1809–1882) An English naturalist who is credited with realizing that all species of life on Earth have descended over time from common ancestors.

EINSTEIN, ALBERT (1879–1955) A German-born American scientist who is regarded as one of the most influential scientists of all time. His thoughts on space and time were included in his Special and General theories of relativity.

FERMI, ENRICO (1901–1954) An Italian scientist. Fermi is mainly remembered for his work on the idea of using nuclear energy for the generation of electrical power.

GALAXY A massive collection of stars, gas, and dust bound together by **gravity** in one system. Galaxies range from dwarfs, with as few as ten **million** stars, up to giants with one **trillion** stars. The galaxy in which our local star, the Sun, sits is called the **Milky Way galaxy**.

GALILEO GALILEI (1564–1642) An Italian astronomer and philosopher who played a major role in the early development of modern science. Galileo was the first to discover the four largest moons of Jupiter, named the "Galilean moons" in his honor.

GODWIN, FRANCIS (BISHOP) (1562–1633) Bishop of Llandaff in Wales and author of perhaps the first alien contact story in the English language. Godwin's tale *The Man in the Moon* (published in 1638) also supported the ideas of **Copernicus** and used an early idea of **gravity** in the story's description of traveling to the Moon.

GRAVITY A natural phenomenon by which bodies with **mass** attract one another. Gravity is responsible for keeping Earth in **orbit** around the Sun and the Moon in **orbit** around Earth. The effects of the Moon and Sun's gravity are also responsible for the tides of the ocean on Earth.

INDUSTRIAL REVOLUTION A period of time, mostly during the 1700s and 1800s, when major changes in producing goods and foods had a drastic effect on living conditions in Great Britain. Later, this major turning point in human history spread throughout Europe, the United States, and the rest of the world.

INFINITE This word describes something that appears to have no limits in size, extent, time, or space.

KEPLER, JOHANNES (1571–1630)
German astronomer and mathematician best known for figuring out the laws that describe the motion of the planets around the Sun. Kepler also wrote one of the first-ever science-fiction works, called *Somnium*.

MASS
The mass of a body is a measure of the amount of matter ("stuff") that it contains. Weight results from the action of **gravity** on the mass of a body.

MILKY WAY GALAXY
The Milky Way—or simply, the galaxy—is the **galaxy** in which our **solar system** is located. It is one of **billions** of galaxies in the **universe**.

MILLION
One thousand thousand (or 1,000,000).

NASA
The National Aeronautics and Space Administration. It is an agency of the United States government and is responsible for America's missions into space, such as the *Apollo* missions to the Moon and those of the Space Shuttle in Earth's orbit.

NEUTRON STAR
A type of star that has collapsed under its own **gravity** so that it is almost entirely composed of neutrons (particles with no electrical charge). The density of a typical neutron star is equivalent to the entire human population being squeezed down into the size of a sugar cube.

NUCLEAR EXPLOSION
An explosion from a nuclear weapon that gets its destructive force from the nuclei (central cores) of **atoms**. Nuclear processes are so powerful that even small nuclear weapons can devastate an entire city.

ORBIT
The curved path of one body around another, such as the orbit of a planet around the Sun. The natural phenomenon that keeps bodies in orbit is **gravity**.

PHOTON
The basic unit of light. A photon is an elementary particle and has no **mass**.

PYTHAGORAS (c. 570–c. 495 B.C.)
Pythagoras was a mathematician and philosopher who lived in ancient Greece. He and his followers believed that everything was related to mathematics and that numbers were the key to the **universe**.

RED GIANT
A bright and large star of medium **mass** that is in the late stage of its evolution.

RED SHIFT SURVEY
Astronomers can observe "red-shifted" light from galaxies that are moving away from us. They use it to measure huge distances and create red shift surveys—huge "maps" of the sky intended to plot the positions of galaxies and to discover the large-scale structure of the **universe**.

SOLAR SYSTEM The Sun and all the other bodies bound to it by **gravity**, including the four small inner planets—Mercury, Venus, Earth, and Mars—which are mostly made of rock and metal; the four outer planets—Jupiter, Saturn, Uranus, and Neptune—which are mostly made of hydrogen and helium; and all the minor bodies, such as asteroids, comets, and dwarf planets such as Pluto.

SPEED OF LIGHT The speed of light is roughly 186,000 mi. (300,000km) per second. Light could travel between the Sun and Earth approximately 173 times in one day.

SUPERGIANT The most massive of stars. Supergiants come in all colors of the spectrum, from young, blue supergiants to older, red supergiants such as **Betelgeuse**.

SUPERNOVA The intensely bright explosion of a star that expels most of the star's material into surrounding space.

SUPERSONIC A word used to describe a speed that is greater than the speed of sound, which is 1,125 ft. (343m) per second.

TRILLION One **million million** (or 1,000,000,000,000).

UNIVERSE The universe consists of everything that exists, all of space and time, and all the matter and energy within it. It is also referred to in this book as the **cosmos**.

WELLS, H. G. (1866–1946) An English writer, best known for his stories of science fiction. Along with French author Jules Verne, Wells has been called the "father of science fiction."

WORMHOLE A theoretical feature of space-time. A wormhole is a "shortcut" through space and time, a tunnel that may allow a traveler a quicker journey between two points.

INDEX

FURTHER READING

BOOKS

Space Hoppers by Mark Brake
FutureWorld: Where Science Fiction Becomes Science by Mark Brake and Neil Hook
Eyewitness: Time and Space by John Gribbin
A Wrinkle in Time by Madeleine L'Engle
Space, Black Holes, and Stuff by Glenn Murphy
The Time and Space of Uncle Albert by Russell Stannard

WEBSITES

NASA's Space Place:
http://spaceplace.nasa.gov/

ESA (European Space Agency):
www.esa.int/esaKIDSen/

HOW TO THINK LIKE A SCIENTIST

Here are five tips to help you think like a scientist. When you are trying to formulate a scientific theory:

1. If possible, try to get independent proof of the "facts," as you see them.

2. Think about whether your theory can be shown to be false. In other words, is it "testable"?

3. Try to test out your theory with observation and experiment. Do other scientists get the same results?

4. Test more than one theory—don't simply run with the first idea that pops into your head.

5. Persuade other people to shoot down your theory in flames (in other words, strongly disagree with it). Debating theories, based on evidence and observation, is another key tip to thinking like a scientist.

And remember, there is nothing wrong with being a brilliant scientist. The universe needs them.